How to Read a Nonfiction Book

BY LISA M. BOLT SIMONS

Published by The Child's World®
1980 Lookout Drive • Mankato, MN 56003-1705
800-599-READ • www.childsworld.com

Photographs ©: Don Pablo/Shutterstock Images, cover
(foreground); ST22 Studio/Shutterstock Images, cover
(background); Dawn Shearer-Simonetti/Shutterstock Images, 5;
Tyler Olson/Shutterstock Images, 6; Sergey Novikov/Shutterstock
Images, 7; Shutterstock Images, 9, 10, 14, 16, 18; iStockphoto,
13; Rich Carey/Shutterstock Images, 17; Ermolaev Alexander/
Shutterstock Images, 19

ISBN 9781503823297
LCCN 2017944889

Printed in the United States of America
PA02360

ABOUT THE AUTHOR

Lisa M. Bolt Simons is a writer
who has published more
than 30 books with more on
the way. She's also been a
teacher for more than 20
years. Her books have been
recognized with awards.

Table of Contents

What Is Nonfiction?

Emma needs to research sea turtles. She has to write a report for school. What will she do?

First she finds nonfiction books. Then she uses the nonfiction **features**. These features may include headings, graphs, and images. They help her decide if the books are right for her research. Once she gathers information, she can write her report.

Nonfiction books are different from fiction books. Fiction books are often stories that are made up or did not happen. Nonfiction books are about real subjects or events. They are written using facts.

Textbooks are a type of nonfiction book.

5

Librarians can help people find nonfiction books.

Unlike fiction, nonfiction books do not have to be read all the way through from beginning to end. Readers can choose what to read. It might be the whole book, a chapter, or even a sentence.

Do you need to do research? Do you want learn about real-life facts? If so, reading nonfiction is the way to go.

Library books are organized so that they are easy to find.

CHAPTER 2

Reading What's Real

Nonfiction is a **genre**. It includes any book about real life. There are many types of nonfiction books. Reference books are nonfiction. Informational books and some books about real-life people are also nonfiction.

Reference books include dictionaries, encyclopedias, and atlases. Dictionaries have definitions for words. Encyclopedias have information about many topics, such as places or events. Atlases are maps. People read reference books to find quick facts.

A dictionary is a type of nonfiction book.

9

Nonfiction books about people include **biographies** and **autobiographies.** Informational books are also common. They give general information about a topic. Other types of nonfiction books include cookbooks, how-to books, and business books.

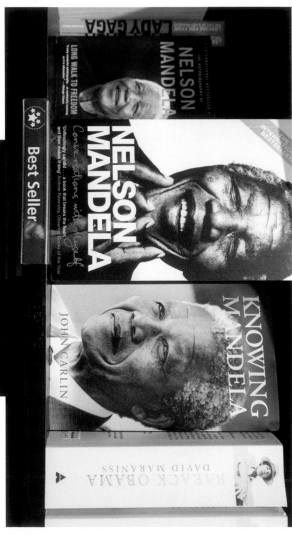

Biographies tell a person's life story.

Most nonfiction books have a table of contents. The table of contents can be found at the beginning of the book. It tells readers what chapters can be found inside the book. Chapters are listed in numerical order. Chapter 1 is the first chapter listed in the table of contents. Chapter 2 comes next, then Chapter 3, and so on. Sometimes the chapters just have numbers. Other times the chapters have titles. Across from the chapter is the page number on which that chapter begins. This allows readers to flip to the page where they want to get information. Other sections at the beginning and end of the book are usually listed, too.

Text and Images

The rest of the book after the table of contents is called the **text**. The text is usually organized into chapters. Chapters may have headings. Headings are like titles within a chapter. They tell what the next section will be about. For example, a book about dogs might include a chapter about puppies. A heading in that chapter might be called "Puppy Food." Readers know this is where they can find information about what to feed a puppy.

Nonfiction books may have images. Images include photographs, illustrations, or graphs. Photographs are taken with a camera. Illustrations are made with paint or other art forms.

Graphs show information using bars, lines, or **symbols**. Graphs can help readers better understand the information. Nonfiction books may also show **data** using tables of numbers.

Atlases have images of maps.

13

Cookbooks often have images.

Images usually have captions. A caption explains the image. It is often found above or below the image. For example, a photograph of a thunderstorm may include a caption. The caption might tell when and where the photograph was taken. The caption might also give the reader more information about thunderstorms.

CHAPTER 4

Additional Features

Many nonfiction books have additional features. These features can be found at the end of a book. They may include a glossary, a bibliography, and an index.

A glossary is like a dictionary. It defines important words from the text. Glossary words are listed in alphabetical order. You will find a glossary at the end of this book.

A bibliography is a list of the **sources** that the author used to write the book. Sources may include books or newspaper articles. Sources are usually listed in alphabetical order by the author's last name.

Bibliographies also include the title of each source, the publisher, and the date the work was published. You can use the bibliography to find more sources. This will help you do more research on the topic.

Bibliographies help people do further research.

An index is a list of topics that are included in the book. The topics are listed alphabetically. The page number where that topic can be found is next to the name of the topic. A book's index is usually longer than its table of contents.

Indexes help people search for topics within a book.

NONFICTION FEATURES

Table of Contents

Caption

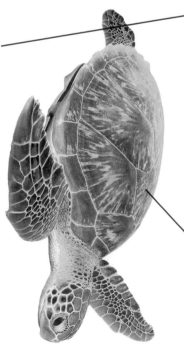

Sea turtles have flippers that help them swim.

Image

Glossary

habitat: A habitat is where an animal lives.

herbivore: A herbivore eats only plants.

omnivore: An omnivore eats plants and animals.

Term

Definition

Index

Want to learn more about your favorite animal? There's a nonfiction book for that!

Reading nonfiction books is a good way to learn about real life. Features such as a table of contents and an index will help you find all the information you need. Now you have all the tools you need to write that research report.

1. **What is a bibliography?**

A. a list of definitions

B. a list of chapters

C. a list of the author's sources

2. **What are three types of reference books?**

3. Which feature defines important words?

A. an index

B. a glossary

C. a caption

4. What is the purpose of graphs in nonfiction books?

GLOSSARY

autobiographies (aw-toh-bye-OG-ruh-feez) Autobiographies are books in which the author tells his or her life story. Autobiographies are a type of nonfiction book.

biographies (bye-OG-ruh-feez) Biographies are books about a person's life that are written by someone other than that person. Biographies are a type of nonfiction book.

data (DAY-tuh) Data are facts or information that help people plan or make decisions. Nonfiction books may show data using graphs or tables of numbers.

features (FEE-churs) Features are important parts of something. Nonfiction book features help readers better understand the topic.

genre (JON-ruh) A genre is a category of literature. Nonfiction is a genre.

sources (SOR-sez) Sources are books or other resources that provide information. An author's sources are listed in a book's bibliography.

symbols (SIM-bulz) Symbols are shapes, letters, or pictures that stand for something real. Graphs may use symbols to convey information.

text (TEKST) Text is the written or printed words that make up the main part of a book. In nonfiction books, the text is usually organized into chapters.

TO LEARN MORE

In the Library

Bodden, Valerie. *What Are Nonfiction Genres?* Minneapolis, MN: Lerner Publications, 2015.

Garstecki, Julia. *Rev Up Your Writing in Nonfiction Narratives.* Mankato, MN: The Child's World, 2016.

Messner, Kate. *How to Read a Story.* San Francisco, CA: Chronicle Books, 2015.

On the Web

Visit our Web site for links about how to read nonfiction books: **childsworld.com/links**

Note to Parents, Teachers, and Librarians: We routinely verify our Web links to make sure they are safe and active sites. So encourage your readers to check them out!

INDEX

ANSWER KEY

1. **What is a bibliography?** C. a list of the author's sources.

2. **What are three types of reference books?** Three types of reference books are dictionaries, encyclopedias, and atlases.

3. **Which feature defines important words?** B. a glossary

4. **What is the purpose of graphs in nonfiction books?** Graphs can help readers better understand information.